My first book of
DINOSAURS

With thanks to Lisa Alderson, John Alston,
Simon Mendez and Luis Rey for their illustrations

First published in Great Britain in 2001 by *ticktock* Publishing Ltd.,
Century Place, Lamberts Road, Tunbridge Wells, Kent TN2 3EH, U.K.

Copyright © 2001 *ticktock* Publishing Ltd.
ISBN 1 86007 267 4
Printed in Malaysia
A CIP catalogue record for this book is available from the British Library.

My first book of
DINOSAURS

Dougal Dixon

ticktock
Publishing

Millions of years ago, the world was a very different place. There were no buildings, no roads and no cars. There were also no people. Instead, the Earth was ruled by huge, lizard-like creatures called...

...DINOSAURS

If the **dinosaurs** and other strange animals of the past **don't live any more, how do we know about them?**

fossils

We can tell what they were like because we sometimes find their **bones in rocks.** These bones are so old that they have **turned into stone.** We call these **fossils.**

6

Sometimes we find their **footprints** preserved in the rocks.

footprints

Sometimes we can find their **eggs** as fossils.

eggs

Discoveries like these help us to **build a picture** of how these ancient animals lived and **what they might have looked like.**

However, we still have a lot to find out about dinosaurs and the other animals of the past.

Dinosaurs came in all shapes and sizes. Some were **huge.** Some were the size of chickens. Some had **spikes or horns.** Others were covered in **armour.** They can all be split into two groups: those who **ate other animals** and those who didn't.

Plant-eaters, or **herbivores,** were often big animals, like elephants, but with long necks and tails.

herbivores

Meat-eaters, or **carnivores,** were often **fierce animals with sharp teeth,** that ran about on hind legs killing other animals.

carnivores

Other animals that lived at the time were not dinosaurs.

There were furry **reptiles** with **leathery wings** that flew in the sky.

flying reptiles

swimming reptiles

There were **big reptiles with legs like paddles** that lived in the seas and oceans.

All these animals lived over 65 million years ago.

Let's have a look at some of the **largest**, smallest, **weirdest** and **fiercest** of these ancient animals.

9

Not all dinosaurs were big brutes. Compsognathus was only the size of a chicken. Even so, it was a fierce hunter.

Its long legs show that Compsognathus was a fast runner. Its long tail helped it to balance when running.

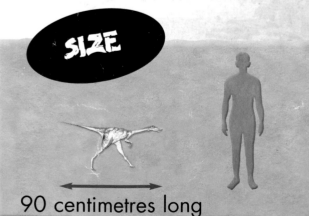

SIZE

90 centimetres long

Compsognathus ate lizards. We know this because we have actually found the bones of a lizard in the tummy of a Compsognathus fossil. Maybe it ate insects as well.

the smallest dinosaur known

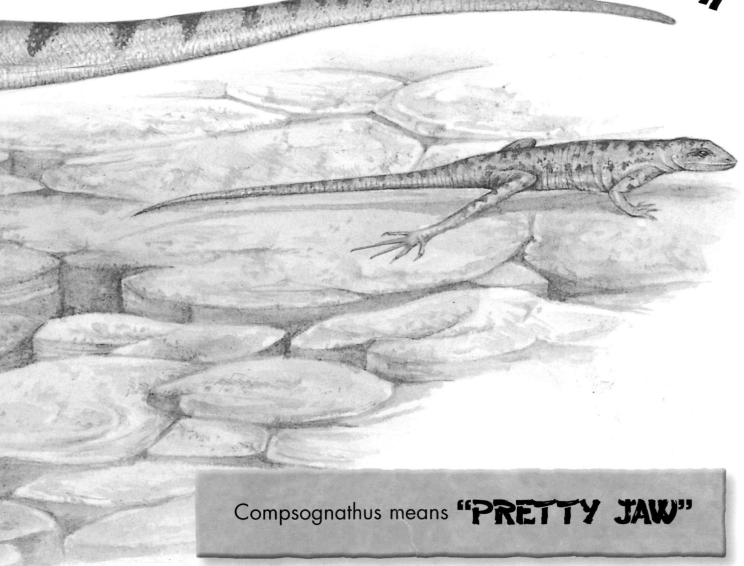

Compsognathus means "PRETTY JAW"

Allosaurus was one of the **biggest** meat-eating dinosaurs. It fought and **ate** the giant long-necked plant-eaters.

jaws with over 70 teeth

SIZE

← 9 metres long →

three sharp claws grip its prey

Allosaurus ate animals that were much **bigger** than itself. It could kill them with the sharp claws on its hands and with its curved teeth.

Its jaws could **open wide**, like the jaws of a snake, so that it could **swallow huge lumps of meat.**

Allosaurus means **"A DIFFERENT LIZARD"**

OVIRAPTOR

Oviraptor was a dinosaur that was a bit **like a bird**. It sat on its nest and hatched its **eggs**, also like a bird. It probably had **feathers** too.

wings that flap but do not fly

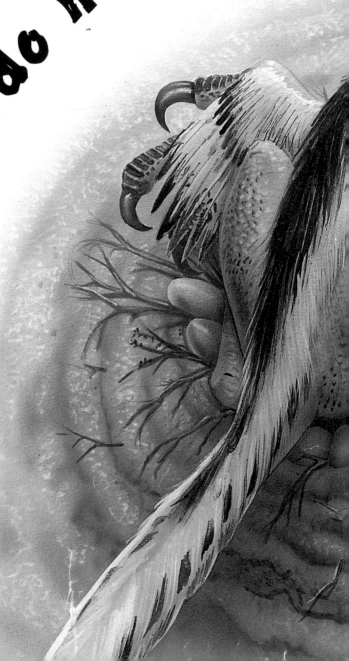

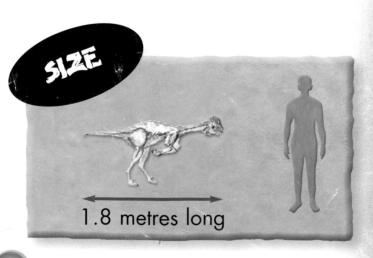

SIZE

1.8 metres long

a crest as hard as bone

There was a **crest on its head,** like the crest of a bird. It might have been **used to signal** to other Oviraptors or to chase away enemies.

Oviraptor's short **strong jaws** may have been used for **crushing snails or shellfish.** It had a beak and two teeth on the roof of its mouth.

Oviraptor means **"EGG THIEF"**

SEGNOSAURUS

Here is an odd one. It is unlike any other

kind of dinosaur. When its bones were discovered,

they confused experts. What Segnosaurus

actually looked like is still a bit

of a mystery today!

sickle-like talons

SIZE

← 6 metres long →

Segnosaurus had **rounded shoulders** and **big hip bones**. It also had **long arms and short legs**, like a gorilla.

Segnosaurus had **enormous claws**. We don't know what they were used for. Maybe they were for **finding food in the trees**, or for **digging into insects' nests**.

covered in feathers like a **bird**

Segnosaurus means **"SLOW LIZARD"**

TYRANNOSAURUS

Tyrannosaurus was probably the most feared dinosaur of all. It was a **huge** meat-eater that lived on smaller or slower dinosaurs. It is often known simply as T. rex.

hunter or scavenger?

Experts are not sure whether Tyrannosaurus hunted other animals or fed on animals that were already dead. It is thought to be able to smell rotting flesh from kilometres away.

SIZE

←—— 6 metres long ——→

saw-edged teeth like carving knives

The teeth of Tyrannosaurus were used to puncture its victim's flesh and rip out mouthfuls of meat.

Tyrannosaurus means **"TYRANT LIZARD"**

Maybe **Tyrannosaurus** was not the biggest **meat-eating** dinosaur. Maybe **Giganotosaurus** was. It was **longer than Tyrannosaurus,** but not as heavy.

Giganotosaurus would not have been able to fight Tyrannosaurus. They **lived in different continents** and at different **times.**

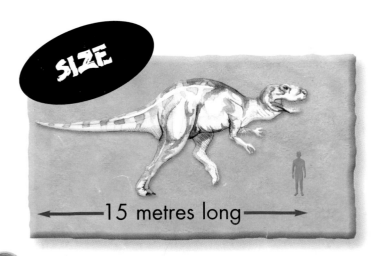

SIZE

←—15 metres long—→

We have not yet found all the bones of **Giganotosaurus** so we are still not quite sure what it really looked like.

jaws that could swallow you whole

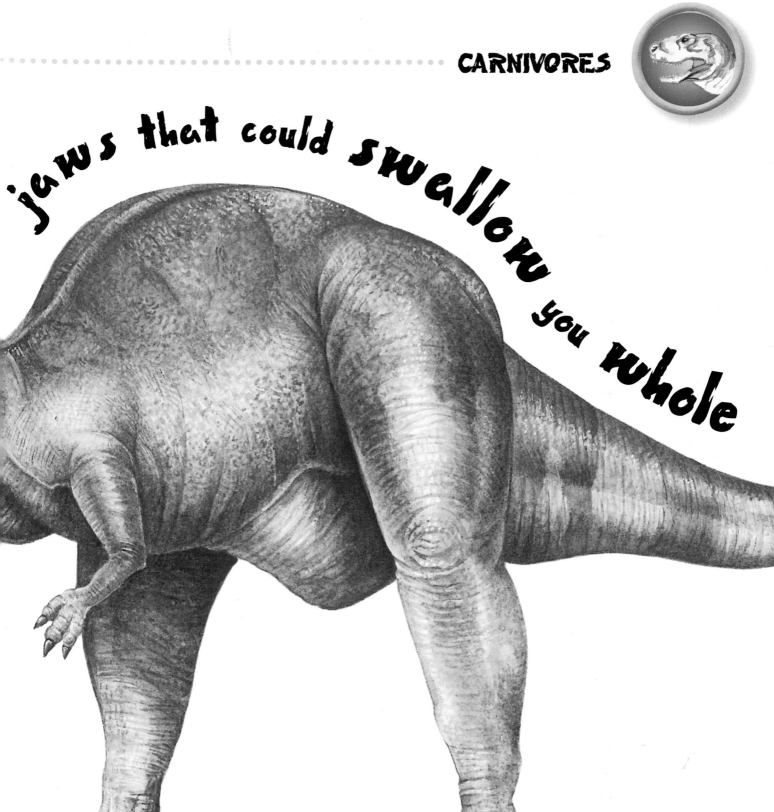

Giganotosaurus means **"REALLY BIG LIZARD"**

Kronosaurus was **not a dinosaur.** It was a **pliosaur** - one of the **big sea reptiles** that lived at the time of the dinosaurs.

Their **streamlined bodies** meant that they must have been **like today's whales.**

a monster of the seas

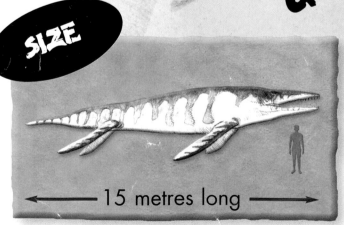

SIZE

← 15 metres long →

Sea animals can be **bigger than the biggest land animals.** The water supports their weight.

pliosaurs had short necks

Kronosaurus had a long head with sharp teeth,
like today's sperm whale. Maybe, like a sperm whale,
it fed on giant squid and octopus.

Kronosaurus means
"KRONOS (A GREEK GIANT) LIZARD"

Elasmosaurus was another **sea-living** reptile that lived at the time of the dinosaurs. It was **not a dinosaur** but an **elasmosaur** – like a **pliosaur** but with a **long neck** and a **small head**.

like a sea serpent

SIZE

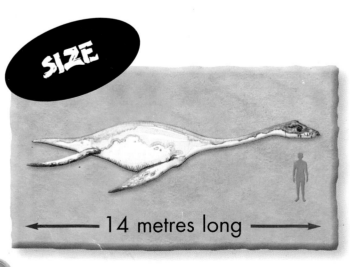

14 metres long

When Elasmosaurus went from living on land to living in the sea, its **legs changed into paddles.** It still had to come to the **surface to breathe.**

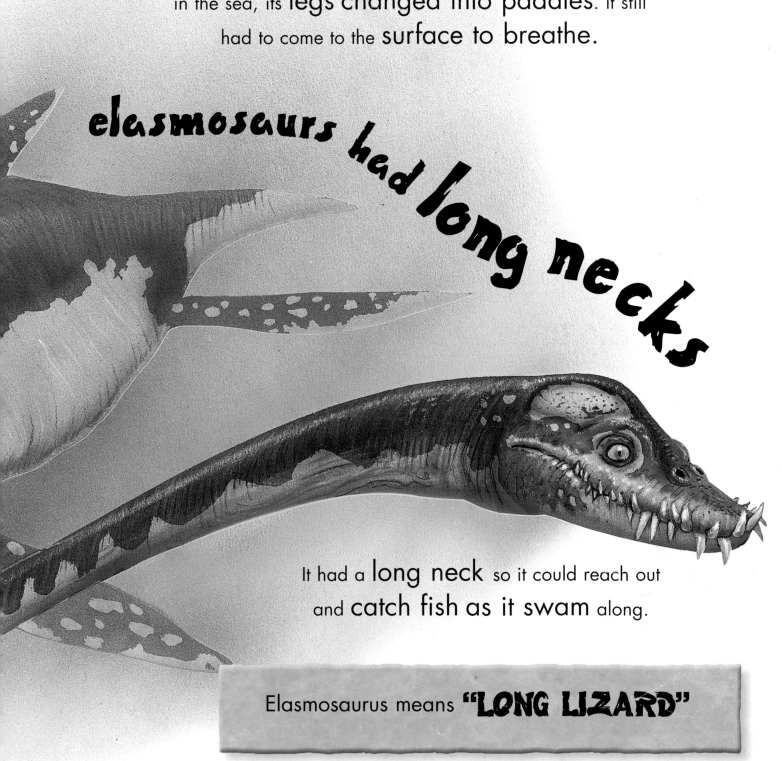

elasmosaurs had long necks

It had a **long neck** so it could reach out and **catch fish as it swam** along.

Elasmosaurus means **"LONG LIZARD"**

Ichthyosaurus was not a dinosaur, but a **swimming reptile** that lived during dinosaur times. If you saw it swimming in the ocean today, **you would think it was a dolphin**, or even a **shark.**

SIZE

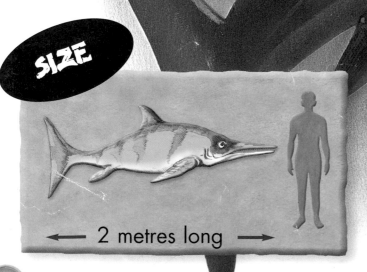

← 2 metres long →

Even though it was a reptile, Ichthyosaurus had a tail like a fish, a **shark-like fin** on its back and **paddles** for legs.

Ichthyosaurus was shaped just like shark or a dolphin. It swam swiftly and chased fish. Also, like a dolphin, it came to the surface to breathe.

it gave birth to live young instead of laying eggs

Ichthyosaurus means **"FISH LIZARD"**

27

Dinosaurs would have been well advised to **stay away from rivers.** There were giant **crocodiles** there. And some of them **ate dinosaurs!**

Deinosuchus was the **biggest** crocodile about at the time of the dinosaurs. It was **big enough to eat dinosaurs.**

SIZE

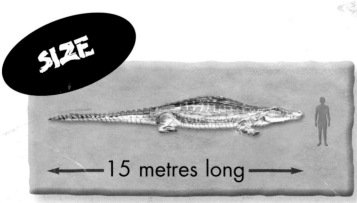

←— 15 metres long —→

During **Triassic** and **Jurassic** times, crocodile-like reptiles lived in the **oceans**, seas and rivers – wherever there was a **tasty meal!**

powerful tail to speed through water

Deinosuchus means **"TERRIBLE CROCODILE"**

Hadrosaurus was one of the "duck-billed" dinosaurs. We call them that because each one had a beak like that of a duck.

SIZE

← 7 metres long →

When it walked on its hind legs, it was **balanced** by its heavy tail.

walked on its hind legs or on all fours

The **beak** was used for scraping the needles from conifer trees. Hadrosaurus had **dozens** of grinding teeth in its mouth **for crunching** up tough plants.

Hadrosaurus means **"STURDY LIZARD"**

The **biggest** dinosaurs were the **sauropods.** They were **plant-eaters with long necks.** The most famous of these was **Diplodocus.**

Diplodocus went about on all fours, but now and again it could **rise up** on its hind legs to feed from **trees.** It ate both leaves from the trees and ferns from the ground.

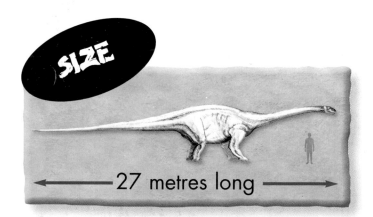

SIZE

← —— 27 metres long —— →

tail like a whip, to keep enemies away

Diplodocus had to keep **eating all the time**, as it was so big, it needed vast amounts of food. It **swallowed stones** as well, to help to grind up the food.

Diplodocus means **"TWO-BEAMED"**

33

STEGOSAURUS

Some dinosaurs had plates on their backs and spikes on their tails. Stegosaurus was the biggest of these.

SIZE

← 7 metres long →

Stegosaurus had a tiny brain – no bigger than a walnut.

tail spikes were used as weapons

The **plates** may have been **used as armour,** or to help to control the dinosaur's **body temperature,** but nobody knows for certain how they were arranged. Here are the possibilities:

flat on the back   in pairs

in a single   in a double row
overlapping row   alternating with
                     one another

one theory even suggests that they
could point towards an attacker

Stegosaurus means **"ROOFED LIZARD"**

Some dinosaurs were **covered in armour, like tanks.** These armoured dinosaurs were **plant-eaters** and **would not have picked a fight.**

The **armoured dinosaurs** had weapons to fight with. Some had **clubs** on the ends of their tails.

SIZE

← 5 metres long →

On Sauropelta the weapons were wicked spikes that stuck out from along its neck. Any meat-eater that tried to attack Sauropelta would break its teeth on the armour, or be stabbed by the neck spikes.

their spikes protected their necks

Sauropelta means **"LIZARD WITH SMALL SHIELDS"**

Iguanodon was one of the first dinosaurs to be discovered.

Teeth and parts of bone were found, and were thought to be from the remains of a hippopotamus or fish.

It was found to be a plant-eating reptile, like a modern iguana – only much, much bigger!

SIZE

← 10 metres long →

Iguanodon was too heavy to spend much time on its hind legs, so it went about on all fours.

It wandered about in herds from one area to another, grazing on reeds.

the first remains were found in England

Iguanodon means **"IGUANA-TOOTHED"**

Triceratops was the **biggest** and most famous of the **horned dinosaurs.**

It had **three horns** on its face,

a **strong beak** for plucking plants,

and a **frill made of bone** to protect its neck.

SIZE

← 9 metres long →

Different **horned dinosaurs** had different **numbers of horns** on the face.

Triceratops roamed the plains of North America in large herds. If attacked, they may have formed a circle around their young, facing outwards – which must have been a scary sight for even the hungriest carnivore!

the last of the dinosaurs

Triceratops means **"THREE-HORNED FACE"**

EUDIMORPHODON

Eudimorphodon was not a dinosaur. It was **a flying reptile** called a pterosaur. It was flying in the sky when the first dinosaurs were walking on Earth.

Even though pterosaurs were reptiles, they were **covered in fur**, like mammals.

SIZE

1-metre wing span

teeth of different sizes to spear and eat fish

Eudimorphodon had **narrow wings** and a **long tail.** Its tail had a paddle-shaped flap at the end, **to help it to steer.**

Eudimorphodon means
"TEETH WELL DIVIDED INTO TWO TYPES"

PTERODACTYLUS

Pterodactylus was the **most famous** of the **pterosaurs**. In fact, all pterosaurs are commonly known as pterodactyls. They **lived alongside birds** for most of the Dinosaur Age.

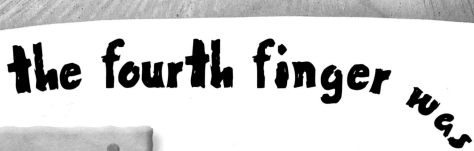

the fourth finger was the longest

SIZE

← 2.5-metre wing span →

the finger supported the wing

Some species of **Pterodactylus** were tiny, with small teeth, and ate insects. Others were bigger, with longer teeth. They ate fish or small lizards.

It had broad wings, a short tail, a furry body and wings made of skin. It had more in common with today's bats than today's birds.

Pterodactylus means **"WING FINGER"**

45

carnivore — a meat-eating animal

herbivore — a plant-eating animal

Triassic — the earliest period when dinosaurs appeared — 245 to 208 million years ago

Jurassic — the middle period when dinosaurs were a dominant species — 208 to 146 million years ago

Cretaceous — the last period before the extinction of the dinosaurs — 146 to 65 million years ago

fossil — the remains of a dead animal that has turned to stone

scavenger — an animal that eats dead animals

armour — special bones under or on top of the skin, in the form of plates, knobs or neck frills that provided protection for plant-eating dinosaurs

reptile   a cold-blooded animal that has scales and lays eggs on land

dinosaur   land-living reptiles that lived during the Triassic, Jurassic and Cretaceous periods

sauropods   a group of large, plant-eating dinosaurs with long necks, such as Diplodocus

pterosaurs   a group of flying reptiles, including Pterodactylus

pterodactyls   the common name for pterosaurs

plesiosaurs   a varied group of swimming reptiles, which are split into two groups; the pliosaurs and the elasmosaurs

pliosaurs   a group of very large, short-necked swimming reptiles

elasmosaurs   a group of smaller, long-necked swimming reptiles

INDEX

PICTURE CREDITS

Lisa Alderson: 10-11c, 16-17c, 20-21c, 36-37c. John Alston: 6-7 stage drawings, 35r and all scale drawings.
Simon Mendez: 4-5, 8cl, 8bl, 8-9c,12-13c, 22-23c, 32-33c, 34-35c, 39c, 40-41c. Luis Rey: 9tr, 14-15c, 24-25c,
26-27c, 28-29c, 30-31c, 43cl, 44-45c.